TRAILBLAZERS

BEYONCÉ

QUEEN OF THE SPOTLIGHT

TRAILBLAZERS

Neil Armstrong

Jane Goodall

Harriet Tubman

Beyoncé

Albert Einstein

TRAILBLAZERS

BEYONCÉ

EBONY JOY WILKINS

stripes

STRIPES PUBLISHING LIMITED
An imprint of the Little Tiger Group
1 Coda Studios, 189 Munster Road, London SW6 6AW
www.littletiger.co.uk

First published in Great Britain by Stripes Publishing Limited in 2020
Text copyright © Ebony Joy Wilkins, 2020
Cover art copyright © Luisa Uribe, 2020
Interior illustrations copyright © Rachel Sanson, 2020

ISBN: 978-1-78895-159-3

Printed and bound in the UK. The Forest Stewardship Council® (FSC®) is a global,
not-for-profit organization dedicated to the promotion of responsible forest management worldwide.
FSC defines standards based on agreed principles for responsible forest stewardship that are supported
by environmental, social, and economic stakeholders. To learn more, visit www.fsc.org

2 4 6 8 10 9 7 5 3 1

Contents

REACHING FOR THE STARS

On 31st January, 2010, at the Fifty-Second Annual Grammy Awards, a young woman owned the stage at the Staples Center in Los Angeles. She was already so famous that she was known all over the world by just one name: Beyoncé.

That evening, in front of a live audience of almost 20,000 music professionals and influencers, as well as over 25 million television viewers, Beyoncé won award after award and brought the whole audience to its feet with stunning performances of two songs. No one could have doubted that the girl from Houston, Texas, was doing what she was born to do.

⋛ A SPECIAL NIGHT ⋛

This wasn't the first time the superstar had stepped onstage to accept a Grammy. In fact, during her relatively short career, she'd already won ten of the special awards. But on this particular night Beyoncé had been nominated for ten Grammys, more than anyone else present, and would take home six – in 2010, that was the most awards that any female artist had ever won in one night.

Beyoncé's Big Wins

→ Song of the Year for "Single Ladies (Put a Ring on It)"

→ Best Female Pop Vocal Performance for "Halo"

→ Best Female R&B Vocal Performance for "Single Ladies (Put a Ring on It)"

→ Best Traditional R&B Vocal Performance for "At Last"

→ Best R&B Song for "Single Ladies (Put a Ring on It)"

→ Best Contemporary R&B Album for *I Am . . . Sasha Fierce*

The Grammys

The Grammys are music's equivalent of the Oscars for movies.
The annual ceremony features performances by famous artists and the presentation of the main awards. Nominations for awards are made by music industry professionals — it is an honour to be nominated and to be asked to perform. Beyoncé is the most nominated woman in the history of the Grammys.

The golden Grammy trophies are in the shape of old-fashioned gramophones, early machines on which music could be played. In fact, the awards are engraved after the ceremony, so on the night of the ceremony, winners are given "stunt" awards as stand-ins for the real thing.

As the announcers read the name of the song "Halo" on the winner's card, the crowd roared in celebration. Dressed in a dazzling silver gown, Beyoncé climbed the stairs towards the stage.

She hugged her Grammy close to her chest and took a deep breath. "I'm sorry, I'm nervous," she said, addressing the audience. "This has been such an amazing night for me and I'd love to thank the Grammys. I'd love to thank my family for all of their support, including my husband. I love you."

MATHEW KNOWLES

For Beyoncé, music is not just a career. It's the way she expresses herself. It's family – literally. The singer's father, Mathew, was her manager for many years. Her mother, Tina, made costumes and styled her. Her sister, Solange, performed as a backup dancer during several of her shows, and has also become an award-winning singer herself. Beyoncé's husband, the rapper, songwriter and producer Jay-Z, has worked and toured with her while pursuing his own very successful career.

TINA KNOWLES

SOLANGE KNOWLES

JAY-Z

That night in 2010 would have been a high point in anyone's career but Beyoncé has never been one to stand still. All her life, she has pushed herself to do better, stretching herself and developing her talents in exciting ways. That evening in Los Angeles was no exception. Even as she accepted the awards and applause of her peers, Beyoncé had plans to take her life in a new direction.

Refusing to be trapped by her success and fame, she took a break from performing for several months and decided to no longer be managed by her father. Her growth as an artist, far from having reached its peak, was only just beginning.

I don't have to prove anything to anyone. I only have to follow my heart and concentrate on what I want to say to the world. I run my world.

INSPIRATIONS

Although many people see Beyoncé as a fresh and electrifying force among music artists, she has always been inspired by those who have gone before. A trip to a Michael Jackson concert when she was a child was an early influence. Later, she admired and absorbed the artistry of legends such as Diana Ross and Prince. Her own success led to her working professionally with many of the people who had fueled her dreams as a young girl.

Diana Ross

Singer Diana Ross was born on 26th March, 1944, in Michigan, United States. As a teenager, Ross was the lead singer of Motown's legendary group the Supremes. The group performed all around the world and sang the hit songs "Where Did Our Love Go" and "Stop! In the Name of Love". After she left the Supremes, Ross went on to release several solo albums, the first of which featured the anthem "Ain't No Mountain High Enough".

In the 2006 movie *Dreamgirls*, a fictional account of a girl group similar to the Supremes, Beyoncé played the part of Deena Jones, a role based on Diana Ross's career. On 26th March, 2019, Beyoncé joined Ross's family and friends to serenade seventy-five-year-old Diana at her birthday party at the Hollywood Palladium.

Prince

On 7th June, 1958, Prince Rogers Nelson was born in Minnesota, United States. Prince grew up in a musical home. His parents were jazz musicians and performed in the Prince Rogers Band. As a child, Prince listened to his parents and discovered his own love of music. He taught himself to play the piano, guitar and drums and to write songs — he hoped to join his parents onstage someday.

His talent as a singer, songwriter and music producer inspired many artists, including Beyoncé. His R&B and pop albums reached the top of the *Billboard* charts and he won seven Grammys. His highest-selling album, *Purple Rain*, sold 1.5 million copies in the first week. On 8th February, 2004, Beyoncé joined her idol onstage for a five-minute set at the 46th Grammy Awards to perform a medley of his songs. He died on 21st April, 2016, at Paisley Park, his home in Minnesota.

⨟ THE PATH TO STARDOM ⨟

Beyoncé was born to perform. At the age of five, she was already singing and dancing across her living room for anyone who would watch. She copied her favourite artists from TV recordings, practising over and over to perfect her singing and her dance moves. Before long, she was doing the rounds at local talent shows and singing auditions.

At nine, she fronted a girl band called Girls Tyme. It wasn't an easy road for the young performers. The group went through disappointments and its membership changed, but by the time the group altered its name to Destiny's Child in 1996, its members were well on the way to stardom and winning Grammys of their own.

In 2001, the highly successful Destiny's Child took a break to pursue solo careers. Beyoncé was the last of the three members to release a solo album, but when she did so in 2003, it was a huge success. Somehow she also found time to pursue an acting career.

With her life under constant scrutiny from the press, every move analyzed, Beyoncé manages to present a wholesome and aspirational image for young fans. It's impossible to overestimate the global impact this legendary performer has.

On that night in January 2010, Beyoncé's most successful best-selling albums were yet to come, along with her iconic performances at the Super Bowl and Coachella. But the seeds of her future were already apparent in her fierce and fearless stage performances and the ever-growing numbers of fans who loved her boldness and her beauty as well as her music.

CHAPTER 1

A SUPERSTAR IS BORN

Beyoncé Giselle Knowles was born on 4th September, 1981, at Park Plaza Hospital in Houston, Texas, United States. Her name was inspired by her mother's French maiden name, Beyincé, which means "beyond others". When Beyoncé was born, her name was unique, but nowadays there are hundreds of girls named in honour of the original Bey.

Beyoncé's father, Mathew, was originally from Gadsden, Alabama. He had been born into a poor family at a time when African Americans had fewer opportunities because of racism. Despite these difficult circumstances, Mathew worked hard to become a successful businessman. He sold office and medical equipment for Xerox, moving up through the ranks to achieve an important role in the company by the time Beyoncé arrived. Beyoncé's mother, Célestine "Tina" Knowles, was the youngest of seven children in Galveston, Texas. Also a hard worker, Tina was a qualified beautician, with her own Houston salon called Headliners. Not long after Beyoncé was born, Tina returned to work and left her baby girl in the care of Mathew's mother, Lue Helen. Mathew and Tina were supportive and loving, and together they created a comfortable life for themselves and their daughter.

In 1982, when Beyoncé was four months old, her parents bought a three-bedroom, two-storey redbrick home in Riverside Terrace, near Houston's museum district. The house had high ceilings and a spiral staircase, and a beautiful garden outdoors.

Houston was an exciting place to grow up. With hundreds of shops and restaurants, along with livestock shows, rodeos and music festivals, there was always something going on in the city.

⋹ MUSIC IN THE FAMILY ⋸

Both of Beyoncé's parents had entered talent shows while growing up and Tina had been in a singing group called the Beltones when she was in school. Music filled their home and Beyoncé loved to hear her parents singing gospel, soul and R&B songs around the house. The radio was always on, blaring out popular hits. By the time she was three years old, Beyoncé could sing along to her favourites. She liked Michael Jackson's music the most and entertained herself for hours dancing along to his tracks.

My parents used to sing to me all the time. My dad tells me that as a baby, I would go crazy whenever I heard music and I tried to dance before I could even walk.

A Musical Moment

In the early 2000s, one of the most popular genres of music was rhythm and blues, known as R&B. The musical movement had originated in the 1940s, when African American artists began playing upbeat bluesy-jazz tunes, with a strong beat and soulful vocals. Some early R&B groups include the Cardinals, the Swallows and the Clovers.

Over the years, R&B evolved to include soul and funk music. Today, music referred to as R&B sounds very different from the songs of the 1940s. Many R&B performers have been influenced by other genres, including hip-hop and pop, creating the styles of artists including Usher, Alicia Keys and Jennifer Hudson. The Grammys introduced an award for Best R&B Song in 1969.

THE SWALLOWS

One day, Beyoncé's parents surprised her with life-changing news: she was going to see her idol, Michael Jackson, in concert! The wait was torture but when the day finally arrived, Tina helped Beyoncé pick a special outfit and get ready.

One of the youngest in the stadium, Beyoncé took her seat and waited for Michael to arrive onstage. Finally, the opening act ended, the lights dimmed and her idol stepped out. When Beyoncé saw the "King of Pop" it triggered a passion for performance that would change her life forever.

"If it wasn't for Michael Jackson, I would never ever have performed…"
Beyoncé

Michael waved a silver-gloved hand, moonwalked across the stage on his tiptoes and sang his most popular songs, including "Thriller", "Billie Jean" and "Beat It". Beyoncé mouthed the words along with him and tried to memorize his moves. When she got home, she imitated what she'd seen onstage.

SISTERLY LOVE

When Beyoncé was five, the family moved again. Their new home was in Houston's upscale and predominantly African American neighbourhood of Third Ward, one of six historical districts in the southeast part of the large city. Not long after the family settled in, Beyoncé's younger sister, Solange Piaget Knowles, was born on 24th June, 1986. Beyoncé liked to help look after her sister, bathing, dressing and feeding Solange alongside her mother.

As soon as Solange could keep up, the girls began to play together and got into all kinds of mischief, but they didn't argue much. On one occasion, Beyoncé came into her room to find toys scattered across the floor. She knew right away who the culprit was, but when she asked her little sister about the mess, Solange denied it! Beyoncé was annoyed, but as she liked having a younger sister to look after, she didn't stay cross at Solange for long.

The girls had a tight bond and respected each other's differences. Beyoncé was shy and introverted, whereas Solange was outgoing and enjoyed socializing and meeting new people.

⋝ STRUGGLES AT SCHOOL ⋜

Beyoncé attended St Mary's Elementary, a private Catholic school with an extensive music programme. Beyoncé was excited to start lessons but hesitant about joining other students, as she hadn't spent much time around children her age. She found it hard to fit in and felt too shy to raise her hand during lessons.

> Every morning when the teacher would take roll call, I wanted to crawl under my desk.

Her classmates could be unkind, teasing her about her unusual name and the fact that she spent so much time by herself. They also made fun of the way she looked, calling her "ugly" and "chubby" and laughing at the shape of her ears. "When I was little, my head was smaller and I looked like I had big Dumbo ears," Beyoncé later said.

Maths was a struggle and one of her fellow students told Beyoncé she was stupid when she couldn't work out the answer to an equation. Beyoncé tried to ignore the comments and focus on the positive things about school life, like dance classes and singing in the choir, but the name-calling got to her. Tina and Mathew soon noticed that she wasn't being invited to birthday parties or sleepovers and that she never talked about her friends. They became worried that she had none.

⇒ A FIRST PERFORMANCE ⇐

Despite her shyness, Beyoncé did not go unnoticed. Her teacher Darlette Johnson watched her seven-year-old student practising alone during dance classes. She could see the little girl had real talent. One day after the lesson, Darlette began humming a song while cleaning up the studio. Beyoncé, waiting for her lift home, hummed along too. When Darlette reached the highest notes in the song, she heard Beyoncé hit each note right on key! Darlette asked her student to sing another tune and Beyoncé's clear, strong voice filled the room. That was when the teacher realized just how talented Beyoncé was. "She can sing. She can really sing!" Darlette said to Mathew and Tina when they arrived to pick up their daughter.

The school was sponsoring a local talent show and Darlette thought Beyoncé should enter. Mathew and Tina agreed it was a great idea. It would mostly be teenagers performing and Beyoncé was only seven, but Darlette and her parents felt the talent show would encourage her to step outside of her shell. The three of them helped Beyoncé prepare and selected a popular song, "Imagine" by John Lennon. The song is about peace and freedom – emotions Beyoncé clearly felt when she was singing and dancing – so it seemed a perfect fit. She learned the lyrics quickly, along with some simple choreography, a sequence of steps or movements that make up a dance routine.

Backstage at the talent show, Beyoncé sang scales to warm up her voice and paced back and forth to calm her nerves. "She would literally have tears in her eyes," Darlette later said about Beyoncé's early performances. "I would have to hold on to her and tell her, 'It's OK. Take deep breaths.'" Once Beyoncé's name was called, she walked out on to the stage. She chose a spot to stare at on the far wall, above the eager sea of faces, and focused on Lennon's lyrics. The room was oddly quiet. In that moment, no one called her chubby. No one made fun of her ears. Every eye was fixed on the young singer as her beautiful voice filled the room.

She spread her arms wide and belted out the lyrics like an experienced performer. Even her parents were shocked at her stage presence! When Beyoncé held the last note, the audience cheered loudly. Several of her classmates who had previously been unkind gave her a standing ovation.

Her first solo performance had been a total success. Incredibly, she won the whole talent show! Beyoncé was overwhelmed with joy, and Mathew, Tina and Darlette were extremely proud. They decided to nurture her talent by searching for more opportunities to encourage her dream.

⋛ THE TROPHIES ROLL IN ⋛

After her talent show win, Beyoncé's parents began to enter her in more competitions around Houston. Over the next few years, she appeared in more than fifty shows, some that included beauty contests. Though Beyoncé was much more interested in singing than in walking the runway, winning in the beauty category helped her become more comfortable with her body image. Tina's mother, Agnèz, had been a dressmaker and had passed her skills on to her daughter. Tina made Beyoncé a colourful, sparkly outfit for each competition. Her shelves were soon full of trophies!

In 1988, Beyoncé's parents entered her in her first national competition, the prestigious Sammy Awards, a talent show held in honour of the entertainer

Sammy Davis, Jr. She achieved first place in the Baby Junior talent category. In her acceptance speech, Beyoncé thanked her family for their support and blew the audience a kiss like a seasoned professional. Her performance landed her a mention in the *Houston Chronicle*.

The following year, she returned to the show and wowed the audience with a mature performance of the song "Home", from the popular movie *The Wiz*, originally starring both Michael Jackson and Diana Ross.

HOUSTON CHRONICLE

A STAR IS BORN

⋚ SINGING ON SUNDAYS ⋚

On Sundays, the Knowles attended services together at St. John's United Methodist Church, a home away from home for many families in the neighborhood. The congregation began with only nine members and, over the years, grew to thousands.

Pastors Rudy and Juanita, along with members of the congregation, supported young Beyoncé by giving her a place to grow in her faith and use her talents. Each week the dance ministry performed choreographed routines to gospel music throughout the service – a favourite part of church for the young Knowles sisters.

Not long after her first talent show performance, Beyoncé asked her parents if she could join the children's choir at St. John's. She loved the tone of the music and how the songs brought the whole congregation together.

⪤ WORKING WITH DAVID ⪤

In 1989, to help eight-year-old Beyoncé improve as a singer, the Knowles family hired David Lee Brewer, a graduate student at the Cleveland Institute of Music in Cleveland, Ohio. Tina had watched one of his performances and, after the show, asked David if he was willing to work with Beyoncé. David agreed to hear Beyoncé sing and was blown away by her skill. "Something about it grabbed me and wouldn't let go," he later said about her voice.

He accepted Beyoncé as one of his first clients and quickly realized he was teaching a star! As her voice coach, he wanted to give her an understanding of musical theory in addition to teaching practical techniques to improve her voice. David helped Beyoncé perfect her mezzo-soprano range, the most common range for female vocalists (see page 45).

Brewer considered Beyoncé to be a prodigy, a young person who has exceptional abilities. He decided to move into the Knowles home to be able to work around Beyoncé's school schedule and he lived with the family for several years. He remembers her waking up every morning asking, "What am I going to learn today?"

As Beyoncé's confidence grew, her talent show wins kept on coming. Darlette entered her star student in several local contests, challenging the young girl to work harder.

> "I put her in some singing and dancing competitions, and it's been history ever since. When I heard her sing for the first time, I knew she was special."
>
> *Darlette Johnson*

CHAPTER 2

A KNOWLES FAMILY AFFAIR

Sitting in the audience during one of Beyoncé's performances were two talent scouts, Denise Seals and Deborah Laday. They were creating a new group and were on the hunt for skilled young singers to audition. Impressed by Beyoncé's powerful vocals, they approached Mathew and Tina to ask whether their daughter was interested in trying out. Mathew was sure Beyoncé was ready for the next step and agreed to take her along to audition.

Although she was a confident performer, Beyoncé had never sung in a professional singing group before and the idea was nerve-racking. On audition day at Evelyn Rubenstein Jewish Community Center, she entered the waiting room, packed with girls getting ready to sing.

WORKING HARD

One by one, the girls went up in front of Deborah
and Denise to audition for a group called Girls Tyme.
Beyoncé gave her performance everything she had,
then waited to hear the verdict. Would it be enough?
Finally, once everyone in the room had sung, Denise
and Deborah read out a list of names.

"Beyoncé!" they called. "You're in." She had made it!
One of the other successful girls was LaTavia Roberson,
a young singer whom Denise and Deborah had worked
with previously. The group began practising right
away. On several evenings each week, Mathew or Tina
dropped Beyoncé off at Denise and Deborah's office.
There, the girls learned techniques for strengthening
their voices and creating harmonies. They began
performing at small venues around Houston and
auditioning for music showcases and TV commercials.

An investor named Andretta "Ann" Tillman
watched one of their performances and thought
that the group had serious potential. She offered
financial backing but wanted to make a few changes
to the lineup and to hire professional producer and
songwriter Lonnie Jackson.

Over the next few months, Denise, Deborah, Andretta and Lonnie cut some of the singers from Girls Tyme and brought others in. The group grew to include Kelendria "Kelly" Rowland, a talented singer and friend of LaTavia's who had recently moved to Texas from Georgia. Kelly's father had fought in the Vietnam War and struggled with post-traumatic stress disorder, a mental health condition usually triggered by a stressful event. The strain on the family had led Kelly's mother to move to Texas in search of a fresh start. Like Beyoncé, Kelly was an amazing singer but shy. The two girls hit it off at once.

Girls Tyme Members

Name: Beyoncé Knowles

Date of birth: 4th September, 1981

Time with Girls Tyme: Beyoncé quickly picked up new lyrics and tricky harmonies, and was the lead singer of the group.

Name: Kelly Rowland

Date of birth: 11th February, 1981

Time with Girls Tyme: After LaTavia encouraged her to audition, Kelly impressed Denise and Deborah with her rendition of "I'm Your Baby Tonight" by Whitney Houston.

Name: LaTavia Roberson

Date of birth: 1st November, 1981

Time with Girls Tyme: LaTavia's big personality and stage presence made her a confident performer

Name: Ashley Támar Davis

Date of birth: 31st March, 1980

Time with Girls Tyme: Ashley left Girls Tyme because her parents wanted a more normal upbringing for her. She became a backup vocalist for Prince, which led to a solo career, a Grammy nomination and an audition for the television singing competition show *The Voice*.

Performing in a group was very different from standing onstage alone. Now Beyoncé had to be sensitive to the movements of her bandmates and work on complicated harmonies. Almost every day, the girls started practising as soon as school was over and sometimes rehearsed late into the night

During school holidays, Girls Tyme sang and danced all day long – even through the hot Texas summer. The Knowles family's living room became the main rehearsal space, but Mathew and Tina also built a deck on the back of the house to create a stage for the girls.

35

When guests came over, the girls sometimes charged a small admission fee and then put on a show!

≡ MOVING ON ≡

In 1990, at age nine, Beyoncé transferred to Parker Elementary School, a school that specialized in music and performance. Studying music was easy but Beyoncé still struggled with some of the other subjects. When teachers asked the class a question, Beyoncé felt like hiding. Even when she knew the answers, she didn't like the idea of walking up to the blackboard at the front of the room with her classmates' eyes on her.

But Beyoncé tried not to let her troubles at school affect her performances. Mathew and Tina spread the word about Girls Tyme, encouraging friends at church and work to go and watch the shows.

Sibling Rivalry?

Solange loved music too. Beyoncé often heard her little sister tinkering on a drum set in her bedroom next door. To make sure Beyoncé and Solange got along, Tina routinely took her daughters to see a child therapist to help them maintain their healthy relationship. Child therapists work with children and parents to help address and treat any social, emotional or developmental issues.

HEADLINERS SALON

Tina offered her salon to the girls as a rehearsal studio. With many of the customers sitting stiffly with their hair in rollers, Girls Tyme literally had a captive audience! Headliners, located on Montrose Boulevard, became a second home for the group and many of Tina's customers became like family. Girls Tyme performed there so often that the stylists had their routines memorized. At the end of each performance, the customers clapped and a few even asked for photos and autographs.

Mathew requested honest feedback from his wife's clients. In general, they were very positive but sometimes they rolled their eyes and sighed as Girls Tyme got ready to perform yet another song!

"In the South in general, but specifically in our world growing up, people were expressive and vivid storytellers. In the hair salon or in the line at the grocery store, there was never a dull moment."
Solange

⋛ *STAR SEARCH* SORROW ⋚

In 1992, all their salon rehearsals and local shows paid
off when music producer Arne Frager saw the girls
perform. Impressed by their talent, he flew the group
out to California to professionally record some music in
a studio. Beyoncé had never been on a plane before and
she enjoyed the three-hour flight.

The girls recorded a new track titled "Sunshine". Arne
had high hopes of getting them signed by a major record
label but first he wanted them to have more exposure
– on television. He got them booked for a spot on *Star
Search*, a popular TV talent show. The girls were both
terrified and excited at the prospect of performing on
TV. They pushed their rehearsals into high gear, learning
complicated choreography, practising a rap song and
nailing their transitions around the stage.

Mathew was taking on more and more of the band's
management and rehearsals could be tense. During one
session, LaTavia missed a note and all the other girls
burst out laughing. Mathew didn't think the mishap was
funny. He angrily told the girls that they needed to do
better. Even though their next rendition of the song was
pitch-perfect, his yelling had spoiled the mood.

Star Search

Star Search was a national television show hosted by Ed McMahon from the mid-1980s to the mid-1990s. Singers, dancers, actors and comedians took to the stage to show off their talents. Many of the show's performers used the competition as a stepping-stone to getting record deals. Some of the biggest names in the music industry made their debuts on *Star Search*, including:

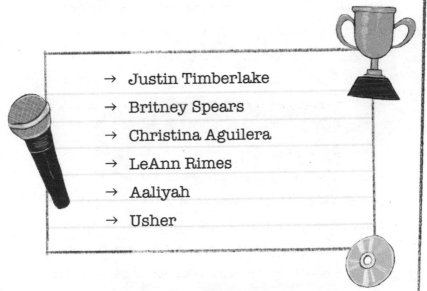

→ Justin Timberlake

→ Britney Spears

→ Christina Aguilera

→ LeAnn Rimes

→ Aaliyah

→ Usher

Backstage, the girls were so nervous they could hardly speak. This was the largest crowd Beyoncé had seen since Michael Jackson's concert and there would be even more people watching on their televisions at home! They stepped on to the stage, dressed in green, purple and white, and lined up like soldiers heading off to war. Beyoncé focused on the lyrics and made sure to stay in step with the others. The music came to a stop and Girls Tyme hit their final pose. When the audience cheered loudly, the girls thought they had the top spot in the bag. Beyoncé was sure they were about to win *Star Search* and get signed by a major record label.

But instead an adult rock and jazz band, Skeleton Crew, won that night. The members of Girls Tyme were incredibly disappointed but the experience taught them an important lesson. Beyoncé realized that "you could actually work super hard and give everything you have and still lose." She also thought that the group had chosen the wrong song – they were singers, not rappers, and their performance had not demonstrated their skills.

"That was my first time I lost something that I really wanted to win."

Beyoncé

Even though Girls Tyme hadn't won, Mathew was proud of the girls for trying. Since they were in Florida, he took the whole group to Disney World. They got to ride roller coasters, eat sweets, play games and try to forget their disappointment. When the episode aired later that year, the girls were sad again, but watching their performance gave them another opportunity to critique their mistakes and make changes. Throughout her career, Beyoncé was sure to watch recordings of every performance; she always strove to improve her routines and avoid making the same mistake twice.

⋛ ALTERNATIVE SCHOOLING ⋚

Though Beyoncé had become close with the other members of Girls Tyme, her parents were worried that she still wasn't making friends at school. They wanted her to learn in a more supportive environment, so Beyoncé transferred to Welch Middle School.

Unfortunately, her experience wasn't much better than at Parker. Her grades weren't improving and even though Beyoncé tried to keep her head down, some of the other students decided they just didn't like her. Her cousin Angie thought that they might be jealous of her looks. She even suggested they might try to cut Beyoncé's long hair – so Beyoncé wore it tied up for months. Though she was still quiet and timid at school, onstage she created an alter ego. Angie named this persona:

SASHA FIERCE

Sasha had a loud and boisterous personality. None of Beyoncé's classmates knew about Sasha but this secret alter ego gave her courage.

Her parents understood that their daughter was having a difficult time at Welch and arranged for a private tutor to come to their house and help with her academic studies. When Beyoncé met Miss Little, her new tutor, she thought that she was strict and the work she assigned was too hard. Beyoncé wanted to become a musician, not a mathematician, and she quickly became annoyed by Miss Little's frustrating teaching methods. Still, Beyoncé knew that Miss Little and her parents just wanted her to succeed, so she settled down and tried to get her head around the topics she was struggling with.

MANAGING GIRL'S TYME

In 1992, Mathew started an entertainment company called Music World Entertainment. After Girls Tyme's disappointing performance on *Star Search*, he wanted to take over the management of the group. Denise and Deborah had already moved on to other projects and Andretta was struggling with ill health. She agreed to hand over the reins. He scaled Girls Tyme back to four members: Kelly, LaTavia, Beyoncé and a new member named LeToya.

BEYONCÉ
- powerful, soulful tone
- confident performer

KELLY ROWLAND
- broad vocal range, which worked well on upbeat songs

LATAVIA ROBERSON
- rich tone
- ability to hit the lowest notes

LETOYA LUCKETT
- ability to reach the highest notes

Voice Types

Most singers fit into a category or "voice type" that reflects their vocal range. These include:

- **Soprano:** the highest voice type for females
- **Mezzo-soprano:** the most common type of female voice, falling between the high soprano and low alto
- **Contralto or alto:** the lowest voice type for females
- **Tenor:** the highest voice type for males, with the exception of the rare "countertenor" voice type, which is even higher
- **Baritone:** the most common type of male voice, falling between the high tenor range and the low bass range
- **Bass:** the lowest voice type for males

Each of the remaining members of Girls Tyme signed contracts with Music World Entertainment. At first things ran smoothly. Mathew made sure they were booked for shows and rehearsed for hours each day. Tina created custom costumes. Each girl had her own individual style, but the group always looked like a unit when they arrived at shows in sparkling fitted tops or brightly coloured matching jumpsuits.

Kelly's mother worked long hours as a nanny and it was becoming impossible to keep up with her daughter's daily practices. The decision was made that Kelly would move in with the Knowles family in order to give her full attention to Girls Tyme. The girls grew even closer, practising through the day and having sleepovers at night.

BATTLE OF THE BANDS

For a short time, Beyoncé enrolled in Kinder High School for the Visual and Performing Arts. Once again, she enjoyed music classes but felt all other subjects were a distraction.

However, one of the things Beyoncé had enjoyed about Kinder was attending the battle-of-the-bands competitions at nearby universities. At these events, marching bands played popular music and paraded around the university's grounds. Beyoncé dreamed of one day being among them and had future plans to attend Prairie View A&M University or Texas Southern University in Houston. Although, in the end, she never made it to higher education, these events would go on to inspire one of her most iconic performances.

⪦ A RISING TENSION ⪧

A couple of the girls struggled with the fact that Mathew seemed to be able to dish out criticism but couldn't take it. If any of the band members complained about his management style or harsh comments, they felt like he disregarded their points and refused to acknowledge his faults.

"Mathew did not mince his words, and it can be tough to take that kind of criticism when you are a little girl. We would try not to let it break us."
LaTavia Roberson

It was a trying time for Mathew and Tina as well. The two began arguing a lot and couldn't see eye to eye on Mathew's business decisions. To take on the group, he had quit his job at Xerox, swapped their large family home for a small flat and sold two of their three cars. "I felt like the group was more important to him than his family," Tina said. The tension continued to build and when Beyoncé was twelve, they decided to spend some time apart.

During a six-month break from their marriage, Mathew moved out of their flat and went to university to take a music management course. Tina worked overtime at Headliners to support the family. The fracture was stressful for the girls. "It was such a painful time that I erased a lot of those memories from my head," Beyoncé said.

≡ DESTINY'S CHILD ≡

The stakes were high. The Knowles family invested everything they had in the success of their girl group. When summer hit, Mathew created a "boot camp" in the local park. He made the girls run laps around the track, singing, so that they didn't get out of breath while performing onstage. He had them practise dance routines in high heels and he discouraged them from attending social events. On one occasion, he publicly scolded the girls mid-performance for going swimming the day before and damaging their voices.

Over the next few years, Mathew worked hard to make the girls successful, trying to book them as support artists for more established acts. Finally, they landed an audition with the record label Elektra.

They wowed the executives with their slick performance and were offered representation. It seemed like the big break they had all been waiting for! They spent the summer at a studio in Atlanta, missing months of school to record their tracks. But at the last minute, Elektra dropped the band. They'd decided the girls were "too young" to progress.

Beyoncé was crushed, as was Mathew. He decided the band needed a more mature image; the name Girls Tyme was now too young for them. The group went through several name changes, including Cliché, Something Fresh and Da Dolls. Inspiration finally struck one evening when Tina opened her Bible and a photo of the girls fell out. On the page it had been holding, Tina read the word *destiny* in a passage in Isaiah, a book in the Old Testament. The girls felt like the word was a perfect fit, and added *child* to differentiate the group from others with similar names.

GROUP NAME

Girl's Tyme (too young!)

Cliché (too cliché!)

Something Fresh (not fresh enough!)

Da Dolls (do we really wanna be dolls?)

Destiny's Child (this is the ONE!)

⋛ GETTING SIGNED ⋛

In 1997, the girls were offered an audition for Columbia Records. The audition room was so tiny that only the four singers could squeeze in and there was no room for instruments. Beyoncé gave the performance everything she had. Then the group returned to Houston to wait for news.

A few weeks later, when the girls were gathered in Headliners, Tina handed Beyoncé an envelope with a local restaurant's logo emblazoned on the front. Thinking her mother was giving her some gift certificates, Beyoncé opened the envelope, only to discover a letter from Columbia Records. Destiny's Child had been signed!

CONTRACT

COLUMBIA RECORDS

DESTINY'S CHILD

Record Companies

A record company, often called a record label, is an organization that makes and sells musical recordings. The company helps musicians with their sound and image, maintains contracts and markets their music by sending it out to influential distributors, magazines and websites. The term "record label" comes from the circular label in the centre of vinyl records, which displays the manufacturer's details.

CHAPTER 3

UNCHARTERED WATERS

A few months after they were signed by Columbia, Destiny's Child released its first song, "Killing Time". It was featured in *Men in Black*, a sci-fi film starring Will Smith, and word began to spread about the new girl band. Their record label encouraged Beyoncé, Kelly, LaTavia and LeToya to pretend to be a couple of years older than they were, in order to appeal to a wider audience. When their second single, "No, No, No", charted at number three on *Billboard*'s Hot 100 in the United States, Columbia Records knew they had made a good decision in signing the group.

Record Charts

The main record chart in the
United States is published
weekly by *Billboard* magazine.
To calculate a song ranking,
Billboard takes into account
the number of sales, the number
of downloads and the number of
times the song has been played
on the radio. It's difficult
to estimate the sales needed
for a single to reach the
chart, because the position is
determined by so many different
factors, including how well other
artists are performing that week.

Reaching gold, platinum or even
multi-platinum is the ultimate
goal for many artists in the
music industry. To reach gold, an
album has to sell 500,000 copies;
platinum, 1 million copies; and
multi-platinum, 2 million copies.

⋜ ON THE RISE ⋜

One afternoon Beyoncé and Kelly were driving along,
listening to a popular Houston radio station when "No,
No, No" started playing through the speakers. They
turned up the volume as loud as it would go and belted
out the lyrics. The girls celebrated all the way home –
it would be the first of thousands of times their music
was played on the radio.

Things were looking up in Beyoncé's personal life too. Mathew and Tina had managed to settle their differences and her father moved back into the family home.

As the band started work on its first album, Mathew wanted all the girls to be involved in the songwriting process. Beyoncé enjoyed putting together lyrics and much of her inspiration came from conversations about love and heartbreak that she overheard at Headliners.

"Women in a hair salon are more open than men in a barber shop."
Beyoncé

One year later, in 1998, Destiny's Child released its first album, a mix of romantic ballads and dance tunes. The album, called *Destiny's Child*, sold half a million copies within the first few weeks – not enough to set the world alight but enough to encourage the group that they were on the right track. Their album release was followed by a few months of performances and a tour supporting Boyz II Men, one of the biggest R&B bands in the United States. From Nashville to Los Angeles, Seattle to Washington, DC, the girls sang at a new venue most nights, before setting off on their tour bus for the next city the following morning. Though the tour was exhausting, Beyoncé enjoyed staying at fancy hotels and ordering room service with her friends every night.

The next year the girls joined R&B group TLC on tour as an opening act. Destiny's Child carefully selected three of its most popular songs to perform: "Independent Women", "No, No, No", and "Jumpin', Jumpin'". On the night of their first performance in Toronto, Canada, as the bands waited backstage, Beyoncé walked up to TLC band members T-Boz, Left Eye and Chilli, to thank them for "one of the best times" in her life. They formed a circle and prayed together before Destiny's Child strutted on to the stage, ready to perform in front of the roaring crowd.

After each performance, there was a meet-and-greet with fans. With the final autographs signed and pictures taken, the girls spent time together on their tour bus, snacking on junk food and gossiping about the show. The beds were stacked on top of each other like Lego but the teens didn't mind. To them, it felt like a fun sleepover every night.

THE WRITING'S ON THE WALL

In 1999, Destiny's Child recorded a second album, *The Writing's on the Wall*. In this collection, Beyoncé's lyrics got more personal and many of the songs focused on empowering women or finding love. She sang the lead vocals on most of the tracks, occasionally sharing them with Kelly. LaTavia and LeToya generally sang the backing vocals but sometimes Beyoncé or Kelly recorded those parts too.

LaTavia and LeToya disagreed with Mathew's management style and felt that Beyoncé and Kelly got more time in the spotlight while they were left in the background. To them, it seemed clear there was a divide between the group members who lived in the Knowles family home and those who didn't. Onstage, LaTavia and LeToya felt they were always in the shadow of the other singers, given fewer solos and positioned at the back during the dance routines. The two claimed Mathew wasn't looking out for all the girls' best interests and they demanded answers from him. Rehearsals became tense, especially when nothing seemed to change regarding who was landing the big solos or best stage positions.

But LaTavia and LeToya continued to struggle. They called all of the girls together and suggested that they consider new management – they wanted Mathew out. Beyoncé and Kelly were happy with Mathew and they trusted his judgment. It seemed they were at an impasse.

LaTavia and LeToya contacted a mediator, someone who could talk business on their behalf. LaTavia's mother, who chaperoned the girls at times, didn't agree with the decision to seek outside advice but the girls proceeded anyway. Beyoncé and Kelly didn't want to be involved. They loved LaTavia and LeToya, but were comfortable letting Mathew handle the business side of things so they could remain focused on the music.

We need a change. This isn't working for all of us and we're a group, right? We have to do this together.

When Destiny's Child's next single was released, LaTavia and LeToya noticed that their vocals weren't on the track. They had recorded "Say My Name" along with Beyoncé and Kelly in the studio, but Mathew had decided to find new singers, Michelle Williams and Farrah Franklin, to record over their parts.

LaTavia and LeToya felt they were being punished for voicing their concerns and filed a lawsuit against Mathew for breaching their contract. They reached a settlement before the case went to court and both girls were awarded thousands of dollars in compensation. There are differing accounts of the circumstances that led to their departure, but however it happened, LaTavia and LeToya were out, and Michelle and Farrah were in.

"Say My Name" was the group's biggest hit so far. It won Destiny's Child its first two Grammys and stayed on the charts for an impressive thirty-two weeks. Still, Beyoncé's happiness at their hard-won success was dampened as tabloid newspapers and gossip websites blamed her for the issues within the group. Upset by this negative publicity, she withdrew from her family and friends and struggled to come to terms with the dark side of fame.

Beyoncé sometimes struggled with bouts of intense sadness she couldn't explain. There were even days when she had difficulty leaving her bedroom. With therapy and support, Beyoncé found ways to cope with her depression while on the road and music became an outlet in her lowest moments.

"I didn't eat. I stayed in my room.
I was in a really bad place in life."
Beyoncé

Depression

Depression is a mood disorder. It causes symptoms that negatively affect your thinking and feeling. Often, people with depression have a difficult time performing common daily tasks, like eating, working, and socializing. People who experience these or other symptoms of depression should talk to a doctor or other health care provider. Symptoms include:

- Feeling sad
- Feeling extremely tired
- Lacking concentration
- Losing interest in activities you used to enjoy
- Sleeping less or more than usual
- Feeling irritable or grumpy
- Feeling guilty

A NEW LINEUP

After just five months with the band, Farrah left
Destiny's Child. The exact reason for her swift
departure is unknown. Some sources suggest that
Farrah missed one too many practices and was
dismissed from the group while others state that she
disagreed with Mathew's management style and left
of her own accord. Either way, the quartet was down
to a trio.

The shakeup was a shift in the chemistry at first.
The four original members had been close friends,
constantly together, but it didn't take long for the
trio to adjust to the new group dynamic. Beyoncé
and Kelly welcomed Michelle and helped her to catch
up with the choreography. They started rehearsing
new music straightaway and their voices sounded
like magic together. This was a new opportunity to
reinvent themselves.

> "It's been wonderful. In two weeks, we were shooting the 'Say My Name' video. We've been shooting up toward the sky ever since."
> *Michelle Williams*

Michelle Williams

Born 23rd July, 1980, Michelle loved music from a young age. When she was seven years old, she sang "Blessed Assurance" in front of her entire church congregation. Unlike Beyoncé, Michelle wasn't always sure she wanted to be a professional singer, so she attended Illinois State University to study criminal justice, but she left before she graduated to turn her attention back to the music industry. Before joining Beyoncé and Kelly, Michelle provided backing vocals for R&B singer Monica.

⋛ STUDIO SESSIONS ⋚

When recording at the studio, Beyoncé, Kelly and Michelle took turns reading lyrics, practising refrains and offering each other critiques. Beyoncé in particular took an interest in the technical side of things – she wanted to understand what sounded good and how to make it happen. Sometimes, they sang one phrase over and over again until it was just right. In 2000, their new single "Independent Women" shot straight to the top of the *Billboard* charts for eleven consecutive weeks, setting a record for the longest-running number one song by a girl group.

⋛ SURVIVOR ⋚

In 2001, Beyoncé, Kelly and Michelle visited a radio station. Live on air, the show's host teased the girls about who would be leaving next. The host compared their group to the television show *Survivor*, where contestants live on a deserted island, with one member voted off each week. With Farrah's dismissal still fresh, the joke hit too close to home. Destiny's Child wanted to present like a strong, solid family and digs about their instability stung. But rather than let it get her down, Beyoncé used the snide joke as inspiration for one of the group's biggest hit songs, "Survivor". She put a positive spin on a negative comment, coming up with the powerful lyrics: "I'm a survivor, I'm not gon' give up, I'm not gon' stop, I'm gon' work harder".

When Columbia Records released Destiny's Child's third album, *Survivor*, on 1st May, 2001, it debuted at number one on the *Billboard* chart. In just the first week of its release, the album sold 663,000 copies!

Oops!

During the filming for the "Survivor"
video, Beyoncé and the rest of the group
were put to the test. Temperatures were at
a record low in Los Angeles but the video
shoot called for a beach scene. That meant
they had to brave the cold and step into
the freezing water. They were so chilly
that it was hard to keep their teeth from
chattering when they were singing! They
tried to make the best of the day and even
enjoyed a few laughs. When a helicopter
flew too low, Kelly's wig flew off,
sending all three members running along
the beach to retrieve it!

CHAPTER 4

OFF THE CHARTS

Destiny's Child earned a Grammy for *Survivor*, but some of the messages in the lyrics caused a stir and LaTavia and LeToya took offense at lines such as:

"Now that you're outta my life, I'm so much better"
and
*"Thought I wouldn't sell without you,
sold nine million."*

They filed another lawsuit, arguing that the song was disparaging and that it should never be played again. Many people thought that the lawsuit would be the end of Destiny's Childs but it was eventually settled quietly, with all parties coming to an agreement. It was another difficult time for Beyoncé, as once again many journalists pointed fingers in her direction, blaming her for causing the drama.

BOOTYLICIOUS

Not long after the release of "Survivor", Destiny's Child was on a long plane flight to London, when the word "bootylicious" popped into Beyoncé's head. She began scribbling down lyrics, writing a song that celebrated full-figured women and encouraged all women to embrace their body sizes. She apprehensively shared her song with the other members. Kelly and Michelle loved the concept and later in 2001 the girls released their hit single.

Over the following years, the term "bootylicious" became so commonly used that in 2004 the *Oxford English Dictionary* added the word to its pages.

I don't think you're ready
    for this
'Cause my body's too bootylicious
    for ya, babe

Destiny's Child was invited to open the Seventh Annual Soul Train Lady of Soul Awards at the Santa Monica Civic Auditorium. Although the event was usually a celebration, the night Destiny's Child opened the show, there was a sombre feeling lingering in the air. Just a few days before, on 25th August, 2001, after shooting a music video, twenty-two-year-old R&B singer Aaliyah boarded a flight in the Bahamas but never made it off the island. The plane crashed and caught fire near the runway. The pilot and all nine passengers, including Aaliyah, were killed.

Her presence was missed during the awards show. Beyoncé, Kelly and Michelle sang "Emotion" to pay homage to Aaliyah, whose music touched some of the same fans.

"She was so sweet, always. She was one of the most beautiful people on the inside and out."
Beyoncé

9/11 Attacks

On 11th September, 2001, a terrorist
group called al-Qaeda hijacked four
passenger planes and deliberately crashed
them into buildings in the United States.
Two of the planes crashed into the Twin
Towers of the World Trade Center in
New York City. A third plane hit the
Pentagon in Washington, DC. Passengers
tried to retake control of the fourth
plane from the hijackers, but it crashed
in Shanksville, Pennsylvania. In total
2,977 people were killed. The attack
shocked the world and still raises strong
emotions today.

⋛ NEW PROJECTS ⋚

After the attacks on the World Trade Center, Destiny's Child made the difficult decision to cancel the rest of its world tour on the grounds that it was too dangerous to travel. Though she was devastated about letting her fans down, cancelling the tour freed up Beyoncé's time and allowed her to try something new – acting.

Mathew presented her with a script for a TV movie, a hip-hop remake of *Carmen*, an 1875 classic Georges Bizet opera. The lead female character is an aspiring actress named Carmen, trying to make her way in Hollywood. Carmen uses her beauty and cunning to charm two men who should be off-limits to her. Beyoncé's interest was piqued; she liked the idea of acting and the role would stretch her as an artist. Carmen was worldly and sly, whereas Beyoncé had a sheltered upbringing. She would need to dig deep to find her way into this character's head. Beyoncé attended auditions then waited to hear if she had been given the role.

Carmen: A Hip Hop
SCRIPT

Carmen: I won't be he..
See I have dr

Blaze: I wanna hear

Carmen: *[sucks teeth]*
No, you don't.

Blaze: No, really. I'

Carmen: Really?

A few weeks later, the call she had been hoping for came. The producers had decided Beyoncé was perfect for the role! Filming with seasoned actors was thrilling. Beyoncé liked getting to know her costars, as well as those working behind the scenes. Although she met lots of new people at every show with Destiny's Child, she never got to talk for long. A concert stop lasted only a few hours and the singers were often rushed back on to their tour bus immediately after the performance. Beyoncé enjoyed spending time with the other young actors, even if she did feel very uncomfortable performing her first on-screen kiss!

Besides Kelly and Michelle, I'm not around people our age for more than forty-five minutes. So I was around people my age for a month and a half and I made friends. So it was way more than a movie for me.

After the release of *Carmen: A Hip Hopera*, she continued searching for roles to help her grow as an artist. Over the next few years, she appeared in *Austin Powers in Goldmember* (2002) and *The Fighting Temptations* (2003).

AUSTIN POWERS IN GOLDMEMDER

CARMEN: A HIP HOPERA

THE FIGHTING TEMPTATIONS

In 2002, Destiny's Child set out on its first world tour. Everyone in the Knowles camp helped to prepare, including Beyoncé's younger sister. When one of the backup dancers had to leave the tour early, Solange, a classically trained ballet dancer, stepped in.

"She was and is such a role model, but I think more so it was an insane learning process for me to have a big sister like that — to be able to see the good, the bad and everything in between that comes with fame and success, and to know what I was getting myself into."

Solange

No longer a small-town group, Destiny's Child had a
list of requests for each venue, known as a rider:

Destiny's Child:
Dressing Room Rider

- six bottles of iced tea
- fine china and dinnerware
  (no plastic cups)
- a selection of sodas
- chips and salsa
- fresh fruit
- deli tray (no pork)
- lemons, honey and fresh ginger
  (VERY IMPORTANT)
- spring water
- fresh flowers
- soap and towels
- two strawberry candles

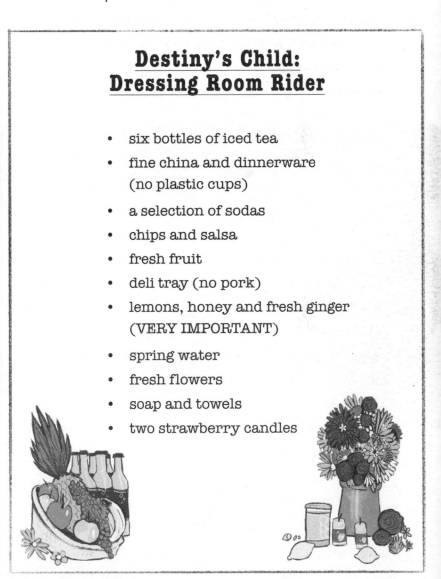

OUT OF THE SPOTLIGHT

Between creating new music, performing with Destiny's Child and appearing in movies, Beyoncé was incredibly busy. However, she tried to get back to Houston as often as she could to spend time with her family and visit her childhood church.

Around this time, she became close to hip-hop artist Jay-Z. The two had met at various events over the previous few years and exchanged numbers at a photo shoot. Jay-Z was twelve years older than Beyoncé but she liked him right from the start. Though Jay-Z was based in Fort Lee, New Jersey, over 2,600 kilometres away from Beyoncé's Houston home, the pair kept in regular contact and were soon calling each other every day. As they grew closer, Beyoncé and Jay-Z met up as often as their schedules allowed and enjoyed going to movies together or simply hanging out and listening to music. Even as love blossomed, the couple was very private about the relationship and repeatedly denied that they were an item to the newspapers. Beyoncé didn't want the press speculating about her love life and was determined never to be photographed with Jay-Z.

Jay-Z

Rapper Jay-Z was born Shawn Corey Carter in New York City on 4th December, 1969. As a child in the Marcy Houses, a housing project in Brooklyn, he had trouble focusing at school and got involved with the local drug gangs.

To escape the dangerous street life, Jay-Z started rapping and in 1989 he landed an appearance on the show *Yo! MTV Raps*. Over the next seven years, Jay-Z took the hip-hop world by storm, releasing many number one albums. In 2004, he became president of Def Jam Recordings and signed artists including Rihanna and Ne-Yo.

"I never lost sense of who I was, not for a day, not before I had a record deal and certainly not after."

Jay-Z

In 2002, Destiny's Child completed the tour that had been cut short the previous year. Fans screamed, danced and sang along in every packed stadium. These were no longer the little girls who had failed to win *Star Search* but one of the best-selling groups of all time.

CHAPTER 5

DESTINY FULFILLED

Beyoncé, Kelly and Michelle had worked tirelessly to reach the top of the charts and by 2002 they were ready for a break. The members of Destiny's Child were all eager to take on individual projects. Fans worried that this might mean the end for Destiny's Child but the record label reassured the public that the band wouldn't be splitting up, just taking some time to work on other things.

A NEW PARTNERSHIP

Jay-Z and Beyoncé released a single together, "'03 Bonnie and Clyde". On the track, Jay-Z sings, "All I need in this life of sin is me and my girlfriend", to which Beyoncé replies, "Down to ride till the very end, is me and my boyfriend." For some fans, this was confirmation enough that the two were dating.

But even with rumours swirling, Beyoncé and Jay-Z refused to confirm or deny that they were together. When asked about the nature of their relationship, Jay-Z told one reporter, "She's beautiful. Who wouldn't wish she was their girlfriend? Maybe one day."

<u>Bonnie and Clyde</u>

Jay-Z and Beyoncé's track was named after
two infamous criminals who travelled
the United States together in the 1930s.
Bonnie and Clyde led police on a chase
across the country, robbing several
businesses and murdering thirteen people.
The two were finally tracked down by
a Texas Ranger in Bienville Parish,
Louisiana, where they were shot and
killed.

INDEPENDENT WOMEN

In 2002, Michelle released *Heart to Yours*, a best-selling gospel album that reached the top of the *Billboard* Gospel Albums chart. The lyrics spoke of her faith and acknowledged victims of the 2001 attacks. Beyoncé and Kelly were featured as guest vocalists on one of the tracks, "Gospel Medley". Michelle won Best Gospel Act at the Music of Black Origin (MOBO) Awards and performed on Broadway.

On 22nd October, 2002, Kelly followed suit and released her own solo project, *Simply Deep*, a fusion of R&B and rock songs. The gold album featured appearances by artists Nelly, Solange and Joe Budden. A year later, Kelly left for the three-week Simply Deeper Tour to promote the album.

"It was a challenge ... I was very nervous, but I came through with flying colours because of my family and, of course, Destiny's Child. There were days in the studio where I would run out."
Kelly Rowland

A SOLO ALBUM

Beyoncé was also working on a solo album. She invited a group of talented writers, including Dr. Dre and Jay-Z, to come together to share ideas. Beyoncé enjoyed collaboration; she listened intently to feedback and opinions about new styles to consider. When Beyoncé was introduced to song samples, initial recordings of a beat, melody and/or lyrics, she listened to the tune several times then rewrote the lyrics so that each line spoke to who she is as an artist.

Although Beyoncé has a hand in writing most of her songs, she has also worked with some of the biggest names in the industry, collaborating with music greats such as Timbaland, Missy Elliott, Rich Harrison, Jay-Z, Rockwilder, Swizz Beatz, Rodney Jerkins and Mark Batson.

The team compiled forty-three songs, of which fifteen were selected by her record label for her solo album, *Dangerously in Love*. Columbia Records was lukewarm about the album and told Beyoncé's team they didn't think there was one big hit on the track list. It would turn out that there were four.

Out of the fifteen songs on the album, the four chart-topping songs were:
→ "Crazy in Love" (number one)
→ "Baby Boy" (number one)
→ "Me, Myself and I" (number four)
→ "Naughty Girl" (number three)

⋛ SECRET SONG ⋛

On 23rd June, 2003, *Dangerously in Love* shot right to the top of the *Billboard* charts and "Crazy in Love" remained in the number-one single spot for eight weeks. With more than 10 million copies sold worldwide, Beyoncé was on her way to superstardom

There was a surprise for Mathew on the album. Beyoncé had kept the last track a secret. It was titled "Daddy" and paid tribute to her father, speaking of their close bond.

You cure my disappointments and you heal my pain
You understood my biz and you protected me

Mathew was touched but not everyone was such a fan of Beyoncé's father. There were rumours that he and Jay-Z didn't get along. It was reported that Jay-Z thought Mathew was too controlling and Mathew resented Jay-Z's involvement in his daughter's work.

When the album was released, rumours circulated about hidden messages – could Beyoncé be confirming that she'd met someone special? And was that special person Jay-Z? He certainly featured in two of the tracks and had writing credits on four. In addition to making music together, the two artists modelled for the cover of fashion magazine *Vanity Fair*'s music issue. The public appearance fuelled romance rumours but both were known to keep their personal relationships top secret.

Beyoncé was proud of what she had accomplished. In 2002, her talents were recognized when she became the first black woman to win the American Society of Composers, Authors and Publishers (ASCAP) Pop Songwriter of the Year award, for "Independent Women Part I", "Jumpin', Jumpin'", and "Survivor".

New Nephew

On 18th October, 2004, Daniel Julez J. Smith Jr was born to parents Solange Knowles and her then partner, Daniel Smith. Beyoncé shares a close bond with her nephew, now known by his middle name, Julez, and babysat for him as often as her schedule allowed when he was younger.

≥ AN EMOTIONAL REUNION ≤

The members of Destiny's Child reunited in 2004 to release *Destiny Fulfilled*. When the trio returned to the studio, they spent a full week chatting about their lives. There was a lot to catch up on – love, solo projects and so much growth!

"The first couple of days we couldn't write anything. We couldn't do anything but talk and eat and laugh and clown. We had the best conversations, which actually became the concept and the theme of the albums. It's all about friendship and it's all about this journey..."

Beyonce

While they were catching up, one of the producers recorded some of their conversations. He felt that the raw, candid discussions would be a good entrée for the *Destiny Fulfilled* album. All three group members had a hand in writing and producing the comeback album and the vocals were fairly balanced, with no one singer dominating. Full of mid-tempo ballads and emotion-heavy pop songs, like "Lose My Breath", "Soldier", "Girl" and "Cater 2 U", the album received mixed reviews, but Beyoncé claimed it was more a celebration of their friendship than a musical statement. Besides, it still reached number two on the *Billboard* chart!

The following year, the trio took the Destiny Fulfilled show on the road. Long-time fans of the group were thrilled. The tour started in Hiroshima, Japan, on 9th April, 2005, and ended in Vancouver, Canada, on 10th September. They held more than sixty shows in Asia, Australia and North America.

The tour was a huge success. Every leg of the final journey was sold out, the venues filled with fans who loved the group. But at one of their final shows, Kelly stepped forwards to address the 60,000-strong crowd in the Barcelona, Spain, stadium:

They were splitting up! As the last song ended at their final performance in Vancouver, Beyoncé, Kelly and Michelle joined hands. When the crowd hushed enough for her to speak, Beyoncé addressed their fans one last time:

"We don't want to get too mushy, y'all. Destiny's Child started when we were nine years old. This isn't something somebody put together. This is love."

It was the end of an era.

⇒ DREAMGIRLS ⇐

Her time as the lead singer of Destiny's Child was over but Beyoncé quickly began looking for new opportunities. In 2006, she appeared in *Dreamgirls*, a film based on the rise of popular 1960s group the Supremes. When Beyoncé read the script, she related to the character Deena, who is quiet and talented. Beyoncé knew she could bring Deena to life but the director, Bill Condon, had someone else in mind for the role. Beyoncé had to complete a screen test to change his mind!

Throughout filming, Beyoncé paused on making her own music so that she could immerse herself in the sounds of the sixties. Though she felt "born for this role", taking on such an emotionally charged character left Beyoncé feeling drained. As with all her projects, she couldn't help giving everything she could to make the movie successful, even at the expense of her well-being.

For her performance, she was nominated for a Golden Globe Award for Best Original Song for "Listen", a power ballad about taking back control, along with a nomination for Best Actress: Motion Picture Comedy or Musical.

⅀ COUTURE. KICK. SOUL ⅀

While she was working on *Dreamgirls*, Beyoncé was collaborating with her mother on a very different kind of project. She and Tina appeared on *The Oprah Winfrey Show* to introduce the House of Deréon, a ready-to-wear clothing and fashion line inspired by the style of three generations of women in their family. Deréon was Beyoncé's grandmother's maiden name.

Agnèz Deréon Beyincé

Agnèz taught herself to sew and worked as a seamstress for private clients throughout her life. She created unique designs, working with embellishments like embroidery, lace and jewelled buttons. In order to make enough money for Catholic school for her children, Agnèz also made robes for altar boys.

The fashion line's tagline – "Couture. Kick. Soul." – was directly inspired by the three women. Tina was the couture, Beyoncé was the kick and Agnèz was the soul. The clothes were hip, wearable and unique. A couple of years later, Beyoncé and Solange launched a junior clothing line. Unusually for Beyoncé's projects, neither clothing line gained much commercial success and she sold both companies after just a few years.

⋛ A POWER COUPLE ⋜

Slowly, Jay-Z and Beyoncé became more vocal about
their relationship. Jay-Z was featured on a couple of
songs on Beyoncé's next album, *B'Day*, released on
4th September, 2006. He also released the single
"Lost One" that year and, in his music, requested more
attention from his girlfriend, rapping "I don't think it's
meant to be, B. But she loves her work more than she
does me."

This trend towards a more raw and open
relationship with her fans would continue over the
next few years as Beyoncé explored new areas of
music and established herself as the ultimate queen
of the spotlight.

CHAPTER 6

ALLOW ME TO REINTRODUCE MYSELF

Paparazzi and fans were watching Beyoncé's every move, with cameras flashing in her face whenever she left her home. The pressure to look perfect was overwhelming and there were some parts of her life that she preferred not to share.

On 4th April, 2008, Beyoncé and Jay-Z invited fewer than forty of their closest friends and family to his penthouse to witness their wedding vows. The space was decorated with seventy thousand white orchids that had been flown in from Thailand. The ceremony was top secret and they had a rule for their guests: no mobile phones allowed. They didn't want any photos from their private ceremony leaked to the papers or social media.

Rather than opt for an expensive designer dress, Beyoncé wore a strapless ivory wedding gown that Tina had created. The couple marked their special day with matching "IV" (the Roman numeral for "four") tattoos on their ring fingers.

The number four is special to Beyoncé and Jay-Z. They are both born on the fourth day of the month. They were married on the fourth day of the fourth month of the year. Beyoncé's fourth album, titled 4, was released on 24th June.

Home, Sweet Home

Both Beyoncé and Jay-Z have owned or rented impressive property all over the United States. Some of their homes have included:

- Tribeca, New York (2004)
  Jay-Z's 750-square-metre penthouse had a large outdoor terrace and was the perfect spot for a small wedding to his bride, Beyoncé, in 2008.

- Midtown Manhattan, New York (2007)
  On the 76th floor of the Time Warner Center building, Jay-Z paid $40,000 per month for an unobstructed view of the magical Manhattan skyline.

- Indian Creek Village, Florida (2008)
  After their wedding, the couple bought a compound on this exclusive piece of land. The home has seven bedrooms and eight bathrooms and is one of only thirty-five homes on the island.

TRIBECA, NEW YORK

- <u>New Orleans, Louisiana (2015)</u>
  Beyoncé bought this converted historic
  church with a mix of traditional and
  modern decor, along with a roof garden.

- <u>Hamptons, New York (2017)</u>
  Jay-Z and Beyoncé can escape to the
  peace and quiet of the Pond House,
  their 17-acre home less than two hours
  outside of New York City.

- <u>Los Angeles, California (2018)</u>
  This $88 million property has six
  buildings, several pools, a basketball
  court and separate staff quarters. It
  was the most expensive sale of 2017 in
  the whole of Los Angeles County!

LOS ANGELES, CALIFORNIA

⌇ SASHA FIERCE ⌇

On 12th November, 2008, Beyoncé introduced the world to her alter ego with her third solo album, *I Am ... Sasha Fierce*. It took eight months for her to co-write and co-produce the collection, and of the seventy songs she recorded, her label selected sixteen – eleven tracks for the standard edition and five more for the deluxe edition.

I Am ... Sasha Fierce was released on two discs to make room for both of Beyoncé's personas. The "I Am" side featured softer, more emotional tracks, like "If I Were a Boy" and "Halo", while the "Sasha Fierce" side was livelier, with some of her biggest chart hits, including "Single Ladies". Despite her success as one of the greatest performers of all time, Beyoncé still felt shy. Sasha Fierce was the opposite and she wanted fans to understand that both personas were a part of her.

I wouldn't like Sasha if I met her offstage... The people around me know who I really am.

I Am . . . Sasha Fierce debuted at number one, making it her third album to do so. It sold more than 8 million copies around the world and the video for "Single Ladies" would go down in music history. Along with two other dancers, Beyoncé performed an iconic routine that inspired hundreds of copycats.

'Cause if you like it then you shoulda put a ring on it.

Cadillac Records

After her album's success, Beyoncé once again took to the big screen, this time to play Etta James in the film *Cadillac Records*. The film is loosely based on the life of record company executive Leonard Chess, a Jewish man who created opportunities for black artists, including Etta James, during the 1950s. Unlike her role in *Dreamgirls*, Etta's part was written with Beyoncé in mind. She recorded five songs, including a cover of Etta's biggest hit, "At Last". Etta was pleased with her portrayal and Beyoncé recalls her saying, "I loved you from the first time you sang."

FRIENDS IN HIGH PLACES

The same year, history was made with the election of the first black president of the United States. Both Beyoncé and Jay-Z were very vocal in their support of Barack Obama, who Beyoncé called "the American dream", promoting his campaign at every opportunity and striking up a personal friendship with his family.

The following January, Beyoncé performed "At Last" at Obama's inauguration ball as the new president slow-danced with his wife, Michelle. Of all of Beyoncé's thousands of performances, this proved to be one of the most emotional and she struggled to hold back tears.

Barack Obama

Barack Obama was born in Honolulu, Hawaii, on 4th August, 1961. He was raised by his mother and his grandparents before attending Occidental College in Los Angeles and Columbia University in New York City. He went on to study at Harvard Law School and became the first person of African American heritage to serve as editor of the *Harvard Law Review*. In 2008, he was elected president of the United States.

⇒ A BIG NIGHT ⇐

On 31st January, 2010, at the Fifty-Second Annual Grammy Awards, Beyoncé's *I Am ... Sasha Fierce* was nominated for Album of the Year, bringing her total number of nominations to ten. It was a star-studded night and she was surrounded by the best artists in the business, including Elton John, Celine Dion and Bon Jovi.

This was one of the biggest moments in her career. She ended the night by earning six Grammys, the most ever won by a female artist in a single night. This record would be matched by Adele two years later.

⋛ GIVING BACK ⋚

With her fame and success came fortune, and
Beyoncé wanted to give back to the community.
Throughout her career, she'd donated vast sums of
money to various causes and been heavily involved in
numerous charity projects. Alongside Kelly Rowland,
she'd started the Survivor Foundation, an organization
that supported victims of Hurricane Katrina, in 2005.

In 2010, Beyoncé and her mother, Tina, opened
the Beyoncé Cosmetology Center at the Phoenix
House Career Academy in Brooklyn, where
recovering drug users could train to become
hairdressers and beauticians. The singer learned
about the work happening at Phoenix House while
researching her role as Etta
James, who'd struggled
with addiction. Beyoncé
hoped to bring a little of the
community spirit that she
had found at Headliners to
these men and women who
were struggling to get their
lives back on track.

⋛ ARTIST OF THE MILLENNIUM ⋛

In 2011, Beyoncé cut ties with Mathew as her manager.
She told the media this was purely a business decision
– as Mathew described it, "Business is business and
family is family." Despite repeatedly stating that they
were still close, Beyoncé later admitted that going
their separate ways professionally had put a strain on
their personal relationship. Around this time, Mathew
and Tina, who had been living separate lives for several
years, decided to officially divorce, further distancing
Beyoncé from her father.

But it wasn't all doom and gloom. With her newfound creative freedom, Beyoncé began work on her ambitious fourth studio album, aptly titled 4. The video for one of the biggest hits on the album, "Run the World (Girls)", saw Beyoncé performing a routine alongside two Mozambican dancers. She had come across a YouTube clip of the dancers' troupe over a year before and admired their relaxed rhythmic style.

She asked her team to invite the dancers to the United States to help choreograph her video and to teach Beyoncé's hired backup dancers their technique. It took months to track down the group, but eventually they were found and brought to Beyoncé's studio.

Though excited by the opportunity, it appeared the group didn't quite grasp how influential their host was. "What's your name?" asked one of the dancers when he was introduced to the international superstar. "I'm Beyoncé," the singer replied, smiling humbly and shaking his hand. Rehearsals quickly got underway. The dance group brought a new energy to the set and Beyoncé was reminded of her fifteen-year-old self, shooting her own first music video.

Her efforts were well rewarded when, in 2011, *Billboard* magazine gave Beyoncé the *Billboard* Millenium Award during the *Billboard* Music Awards show in Las Vegas, Nevada, on 22nd May. Beyoncé wore a long sparkling gown and performed "Run the World (Girls)" on television for the first time. To top off an already special night, Tina and Julez presented her with the award. Onstage, Beyoncé hugged her mom and nephew and thanked Kelly, Michelle, Jay-Z and even previous Destiny's Child members LaTavia and LeToya.

⋸ STARTING A FAMILY ⋸

Though Beyoncé and Jay-Z were ready to expand their family, it would prove more difficult than the two had planned. When Beyoncé became pregnant, the couple was thrilled – but their excitement was short lived. During a check-up with her doctor, Beyoncé discovered that she had miscarried. The devastating news left her heartbroken.

But in 2011, at MTV's Video Music Awards, Beyoncé had happier news to share. Dressed in a white button-up shirt and purple spangled jacket on top, she walked on to the stage to give her fans a surprise.

"Tonight I want you to stand up on your feet. I want you to feel the love that's growing inside of me."
Beyoncé

When her performance of "Love on Top" ended, she smiled, pulled open her blazer and rubbed her baby bump. She was pregnant!

With her pregnancy announcement, Beyoncé nearly broke Twitter! In response to her news, there were almost 9,000 tweets per second.

On 7th January, 2012, Beyoncé started feeling contractions and headed to the hospital in Lenox Hill, New York City. The couple welcomed a daughter to the world and named her Blue Ivy, a play on words, as "Ivy" sounds like "IV", the Roman numeral for their favourite number.

CHAPTER 7

ON THE RUN

Beyoncé took to motherhood the way she had taken to every other challenge in her life. She adored spending time with her daughter, who she thought was the most amazing thing she had ever created. But soon she felt the itch to get back in the studio and on the stage.

If there was any doubt that Beyoncé had established herself as an iconic artist, she dispelled it in 2013 with one of the most memorable Super Bowl performances of all time. In some ways, the gruelling eight-hundred-second set was a culmination of everything she had ever worked towards, bringing together her impressive list of chart-topping hits with fantastic staging and slick choreography.

"I'm a perfectionist," Beyoncé admitted to a journalist, discussing the five months of intense rehearsals during which she'd often finish practising in the early hours of the morning, her feet bloodied and bruised.

Every part of the performance had to be exactly right, from the backup dancers to the lighting. Her outfit, a tight black bodysuit, took two hundred hours to put together. Due to the intense rehearsal schedule, Beyoncé lost weight and the waist had to be taken in repeatedly to ensure a flattering fit.

The set began with an explosion of red-and-white flares and a giant white outline of Beyoncé above the stage. Then the singer emerged to perform "Love on Top". Later in the performance, Beyoncé was joined by Michelle and Kelly, rising up through hidden trapdoors to sing a few of Destiny's Child's greatest hits to the 70,000-strong crowd. To wrap up the performance, Beyoncé turned down the tempo and ended on the emotionally charged "Halo".

The set went down in history. The *New York Times* declared that Beyoncé had "silenced her doubters" and the *Daily Telegraph* called it a "take-no-prisoners assault on the senses". Moments after she had finished, a power cut in the stadium caused a delay to the second half. For many, Bey's performance had literally overshadowed the game.

The Super Bowl
Half-time Show

The Super Bowl is a major championship game in American football and one of the most-watched events on television. The half-time show provides an opportunity for legendary musicians to reach an audience of millions.

One of the most memorable half-time performances was Michael Jackson's headlining set during Super Bowl XXVII. A few years after her first appearance, Beyoncé played homage to Michael's iconic black-and-gold military-style outfit during her politically charged 2016 Super Bowl performance of "Formation".

It wasn't long before Beyoncé was once again sharing new music, with the surprise release of her fifth album, *Beyoncé*, in 2013. Even though there had been no announcement or advertising, the album sold a million copies worldwide in just six days! Beyoncé showcased a different, edgier sound and she recorded an intimate music video for each song, showing many different sides of herself, in her roles as a new mother, a professional entertainer and a businesswoman.

In the video for "Pretty Hurts", Beyoncé competes in a beauty pageant, wearing a sash that reads *Miss 3rd Ward*, a reference to the numerous competitions she entered as a child.

AROUND THE GLOBE AGAIN

Next came another world tour, followed by a joint show with Jay-Z, titled On the Run. For years the couple had talked about a joint tour; each knew how the other operated onstage and on the road. Now, with two-year-old Blue Ivy along for the ride, the timing was right to take the stage together. The artists were on the run but not quite like Bonnie and Clyde, the criminal duo who had inspired their first collaboration. "We're on the run from everything. On the run from becoming a cliché. On the run from doing the same thing again," Jay-Z told reporters.

Beyoncé and Jay-Z kicked off a sold out On the Run tour on 25th June, 2014, at Sun Life Stadium in Miami, Florida, and ended it on 13th September at the Stade de France in Paris. Fans poured into arenas around the world to listen to the top songs by two of the most powerful and influential artists of all time. Images of the couple, their private wedding ceremony and their family flashed on a screen behind them as they walked up and down two long runways dividing the crowd.

⋛ LETTING LIFE IN ⋜

In 2016, Beyoncé released *Lemonade*, her sixth album and second visual project which sold 485,000 copies in the first week. *Lemonade*, which is divided into eleven chapters, was the best-selling album of 2016 and was nominated for nine Grammys.

It seemed that Beyoncé was never going to slow down, constantly recording new material and relentlessly rehearsing for tours and shows. But in 2017, something happened that forced her to stop and take stock of everything. She had planned to perform at the annual Coachella Valley Music and Arts Festival in Indio, California, but she was surprised with news from her doctor that she was pregnant again. Beyoncé got another shock when she found out she was having twins!

Her body began to change and she was unable to perform the energetic dance routines so integral to her performances. She delayed her Coachella appearance in order to rest during her pregnancy and spend time with Blue Ivy.

While she was pregnant, Beyoncé developed pre-eclampsia, a dangerous condition that causes high blood pressure in expectant mothers. Because one of the twins' heartbeat paused a few times, Beyoncé had to undergo an emergency cesarean section. On 13th June, 2017, Beyoncé and Jay-Z welcomed their twins, Rumi and Sir.

I feel like I'm a new woman in a new chapter of my life. I'm not even trying to be who I was. It's so beautiful that children do that to you.

In 2018, her plan to perform at Coachella was back on track. Beyoncé would be the first black woman to headline the festival and she was determined to pay homage to her African American heritage during the performance. Preparation for the set required four months of music rehearsals and four months of dance rehearsals.

"I studied my history. I studied my past. And I put every mistake, all of my triumphs, my twenty-two-year career into my two-hour Homecoming performance."
Beyoncé

Beyoncé wanted her Coachella performance to have the same atmosphere as the battle-of-the-bands competitions she'd attended back in high school. She called the events "the highlight of my year". She wanted her set to be something more than a fun show. "Instead of me pulling out my flower crown," she told the press, "it was important for me to bring our culture to Coachella. We were able to create a free, safe space where none of us were marginalized."

She had a demanding rehearsal schedule, along with a six-year-old and new twins in her trailer. Beyoncé cut out bread, dairy, sugar, carbs, meat, fish and alcohol to meet her performance goals, and pushed her body to the limits of what was possible.

On the Coachella stage, she first wore denim shorts, a glittery hoodie and white tassel boots, before changing into an array of other dazzling costumes. The show included a huge marching band, along with a twirler and two break-dancers. Beyoncé's performance spanned her entire career, including her time with Destiny's Child. She once again welcomed Kelly and Michelle to the stage as the huge crowd went wild. One of the most unexpected moments of the performance was Beyoncé's rendition of "Lift Every Voice and Sing", sometimes referred to as the black national anthem. Her performance was one of the most watched Coachella videos on YouTube ever and became known as "Beychella".

Act 1

1. INTRO
2. CRAZY IN LOVE
3. FREEDOM
4. LIFT EVERY VOICE AND S.
5. FORMATION
6. SORRY / KITTY KAT
7. BOW DOWN

"Lift Every Voice and Sing"

In 1900, author and civil rights activist James Weldon Johnson wrote "Lift Every Voice and Sing", a poem celebrating black unity. At the turn of the twentieth century, though slavery had been abolished, Jim Crow laws were introduced across all former Confederate states, limiting black people's opportunities and forcing black and white people to live separate lives.

In "Lift Every Voice and Sing", Johnson encourages black people to "sing a song full of the faith that the dark past has taught us, sing a song full of the hope that the present has brought us."

In 1920, "Lift Every Voice and Sing" became the official song of the National Association for the Advancement of Coloured People and is often referred to as the black national anthem.

On 17th April, 2019, Netflix released *Homecoming*, an in-depth look at Beyoncé's Coachella set, giving fans an insight into just how much performing means to this legendary singer. The documentary included quotes from influential black leaders and artists who have inspired Beyoncé and her work.

CONCLUSION

MUSIC ROYALTY

After more than twenty years at the top of her game, Beyoncé continues to push creative boundaries. Her family, friends, fellow artists and members of her fan club, the Beyhive, provide a support network, but there's no doubt that Beyoncé owes most of her success to nobody but herself. Her drive, determination and ceaseless striving for perfection have ensured she will be remembered for years, if not centuries, to come.

"In addition to being just a beautiful young woman, she's been a role model and a powerful presence for young girls and women all around the world. I'm very proud of her. I'm very proud of the woman she is."
Michelle Obama

THE BEYHIVE

Anyone with an interest in Beyoncé knows that her fans are some of the most dedicated and organized in the world. The Beyhive is a virtual community started by Beyoncé's management company. It's as busy as it sounds, ensuring that her millions of fans are the first to know about performances, merchandise and music news. In her many award acceptance speeches, Beyoncé is quick to thank the fans who follow and love her.

In 2019, a picture that Beyoncé posted on her Instagram account, showing her facing Nala, the character she voices in the remake of Disney's *The Lion King*, reached almost 2.5 million likes in just one hour.

In addition to books, films and, of course, music records, Beyoncé's merchandise spans everything from perfumes to sportswear. But even with so many different commercial ventures, Beyoncé tries to stay true to who she dreamed of being as a little girl.

"I don't really like to call myself a brand and I don't like to think of myself as a brand. I'm a singer, a songwriter, a musician and a performer. And an actress and all the other things that I do. When you add it all together, some might call it a brand but that's not my focus."

Beyoncé

It's vital to Beyoncé that decisions about the music, images and information she releases are her own. In the momentous year of 2011, when she took the management of her career and her music into her own hands, she showed the determination and directness for which she is well known. She decided to build her "own empire and show other women when you get to this point in your career, you don't have to go sign with someone else and share your money and your success – you do it yourself."

For Beyoncé, it's important to show her fans that they too can make decisions about their own lives.

⋛ PRESENTING HER POLITICS ⋚

As Beyoncé's career has gone on, she has become more vocal about her political opinions. From backing Barack Obama's campaign to referencing the Black Lives Matter movement in her video for "Formation", Beyoncé is using her platform to raise awareness about issues affecting the United States and the world. Through her music and accompanying videos, she hopes to draw attention to the injustice she sees and to make a difference.

Stop Shooting US

Black Lives Matter

Black Lives Matter (BLM) is a movement against violence and racism towards black people. BLM holds regular protests against discrimination and racial inequality, as well as police killings of black people. The movement began on Twitter in 2013, when a white neighborhood watch captain was acquitted of all charges after shooting a black high school student and the hashtag #BlackLivesMatter started trending.

Beyoncé paid tribute to the movement in her video for "Formation", where the phrase "Stop shooting us" is graffitied on a wall behind a young man facing off against a line of police officers.

Beyoncé's story teaches her fans one thing for sure. As much as they discuss and dream, it's impossible to predict what she will do next. Will she tour and collaborate with Jay-Z again? Will she step deeper into the world of politics? Could Queen Bey one day become president?

What is certain is that whatever she does will be her decision and she will reveal her plans when she is ready.

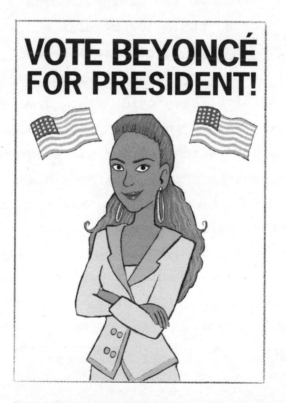

$\approx$ ARTIST LOVE $\approx$

Within the music industry, fellow artists have been quick to praise Beyoncé for her passion and hard work. Over the years, the once painfully shy and quiet child blossomed into a confident leader. She has evolved into a global superstar who continues to inspire through her music, business and charitable work.

"I'm such a fan...
Obviously, Queen Bey
until the day I die."
Adele

"It's like normal for everyone to love Beyoncé but I love her more than that amount, like more than the normal amount...
She's awesome."
Taylor Swift

"I'm always, just like always, in awe of her talent ... I love working with Bey. She's incredible. Whenever she's ready to work, I'm ready to work."
Drake

"Just her name alone defines greatness. Here I am with someone who I admire so much just cause [she's] so driven. She told me I killed it. That really resonates with me."
Nicki Minaj

Over the years, Beyoncé has performed for audiences around the world but her contributions offstage are equally significant. She has supported more than thirty-seven charitable organizations and thirty-three causes, providing aid to those most in need of help.

The BeyGood Foundation supports organizations locally and globally. One of the foundation's projects works with St. John's United Methodist Church to build housing and community youth centres near her old Houston neighbourhood.

"I've known Beyoncé since she was a little girl. She grew up at St. John's... [She] has been an amazing friend and generous supporter."
Pastor Rudy Rasmus,
St. John's Church

One of Beyoncé's greatest strengths has always been her ability to work with others, valuing their unique contributions while having the confidence to speak up for her own views and vision. Over the years she has worked with many skilled producers and artists, launching successful albums and smaller projects.

Everything Beyoncé does is on her terms. Where some celebrities promote their work with endless magazine stories and interviews, Beyoncé has always kept the media at arm's length, allowing the public to see only what she wants people to see, when she's ready to let them see it. Perhaps the most exciting thing about this iconic superstar is her ability to surprise her fans again and again. Trends change, celebrities come and go, but Queen Bey is here to stay.

Timeline

Billboard unveils the Hot 100 chart.

4th December
Shawn Corey Carter (Jay-Z) i
born in Brooklyn
New York.

1958   1959   1969

4th May
Frank Sinatra is among the winners at the First Annual Grammy Awards.

Girls Tyme forms and begins performing together.

1988   1990

Beyoncé sings "Imagine" by John Lennon during her first talent show — and wins.

1981 1986

4th September
Beyoncé Giselle
Knowles is born
in Houston,
Texas.

Girls Tyme signs
with Columbia
Records and becomes
Destiny's Child,
with Mathew Knowles
as the group's
manager.

1992 1996 1998

Girls Tyme
performs
on the TV
talent show
Star Search.

17th February
Destiny's Child
releases its
first album,
*Destiny's
Child*.

LaTavia Roberson and LeToya Luckett leave Destiny's Child and are replaced by Michelle Williams and Farrah Franklin. Farrah leaves the band after five months.

Beyoncé appears in the TV film *Carmen: A Hip Hopera*

2000   2001   2001

11th September
Terrorists hijack four commercial airplanes and intentionally fly them into the Twin Towers at the World Trade Center in New York City and the Pentagon in Washington, DC. The fourth plane crashes into an empty field in Pennsylvania.

4th April
Beyoncé marries Jay-Z.

2006   2008

Beyoncé appears in *Dreamgirls* and releases her album *B'Day*.

The *Oxford English Dictionary* adds the word "bootylicious" to its pages.

Destiny's Child announces that the group will disband after its final tour.

2003

2005

23rd June
Beyoncé releases her debut solo album, *Dangerously in Love*.

20th January
Barack Obama becomes president of the United States.

2008

2009

12th November
Beyoncé releases *I Am . . . Sasha Fierce*, her third solo album.

25th June
Michael Jackson dies at his home in Los Angeles, California.

24th June
Beyoncé releases 4, her fourth studio album.

2010   2011   2012

31st January
Beyoncé wins six Grammys in one night.

11th February
Whitney Houston dies at her home in Los Angeles, California.

13th June
Beyoncé and Jay-Z welcome twins, Rumi and Sir.

2017   2018

14th April
Beyoncé performs at the annual Coachella Valley Music and Arts Festival in Indio, California.

Further Reading

→ *Beyoncé* (Ultimate Superstars) by Melanie Hamm (Studio Press, 2019)

→ *Beyoncé: Shine Your Light* by Sarah Warren and Geneva Bowers (HMH Books for Young Readers, 2019)

→ *Jay-Z* (Hip-Hop Headliners) by Roman P. Nacerous (Gareth Stevens Publishing, 2011)

→ *Music Legends* (40 Inspiring Icons) by Hervé Guilleminot and Jérôme Masi (Wide Eyed Editions, 2018)

Websites

→ Beyonce.com
Beyoncé's official website, with information about her music, upcoming tours, BeyGood Foundation and merchandise.

→ billboard.com/charts
Billboard's current top music charts.

Glossary

alter ego: A different version of oneself or the opposite side of someone's personality.

choreography: The sequence of steps and movements in a dance performance.

collaborate: To work together with another person or organization to produce or create something.

congregation: An assembly of people, usually at a religious service.

contemporary: Relating to the present time.

depression: A serious medical condition that affects how you feel, think and handle daily activities. Symptoms can include deep sadness, hopelessness and loss of interest or pleasure in previously enjoyed activities, as well as changes in sleeping and eating.

<u>Glossary</u>

disband: To end or break up, as an organization or a group.

feminism: The belief that men and women should have equal rights and opportunities.

Jim Crow: Discriminatory laws and customs in the Southern United States between the 1860s and 1960s that restricted where black people could live, work, go to school, recreate, eat, drink and even use the bathroom.

moonwalk: To perform a dance move in which the dancer slides backwards while appearing to make forward walking motions.

pre-eclampsia: A serious condition that occurs in late pregnancy and results in high blood pressure in the mother.

Glossary

prodigy: A young person with exceptional talent or abilities.

protest: An organized demonstration meant to bring public attention to an injustice or a problem.

Index

Index

Index

Index

COMING SOON:

TRAILBLAZERS

ALBERT EINSTEIN

THE GREATEST MIND IN PHYSICS

Imagination is more important than knowledge

PAUL VIRR